A·Q·U·A·M·A·S·T·E·R

——— Today's Essential

GW00992824

KEEPING
GOLDFISH

Bernice Brewster • Nick Fletcher

INTERPET PUBLISHING

ISBN: 1-84286-096-8

PUBLISHING CREDITS

Created and compiled: Ideas into Print,
Claydon, Suffolk, IP6 0AB, England.
Design and prepress: Stuart Watkinson,
Ayelands, New Ash Green,
Kent DA3 8JW, England.
Computer graphics: Phil Holmes
and Stuart Watkinson.
Photography: Geoffrey Rogers
© Interpet Publishing.
Production management:
Consortium, Poslingford,
Suffolk CO10 8RA, England.
Print production: Sino Publishing
House Ltd., Hong Kong.

Printed and bound in China

AUTHORS

Bernice Brewster graduated from London
University and then worked for the Fish Section
of the Natural History Museum before moving to
a company dealing in Japanese Koi. She now
runs an aquatic consultancy. In addition to
writing articles for fishkeeping magazines, she
has also contributed papers to scientific and
veterinary journals on aspects of fish husbandry
and management.

Nick Fletcher is a prolific contributor to aquatic
publications. An interest in tropical and
coldwater fishes stems from his lifelong hobby
of angling, which he still finds relaxing. Mainly,
however, he prefers keeping fish to catching
them, and instead of a lawn he has a koi pond.

Consultant: Dennis Roberts, Nationwide
and G.S.G.B. judge.

▼ *Plastic plants are ideal for goldfish tanks
and will look more lifelike after a few weeks.*

Contents

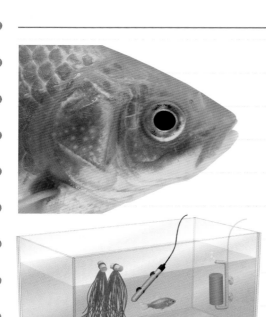

The history of goldfish

The goldfish is probably the most popular pet fish in the world; there can be very few countries where it has not been introduced. Although we know that the goldfish species *(Carassius auratus)* is native to China, there are very few clues to tell us when it was first domesticated. One thing is certain: while the history of goldfish development may appear quite disjointed and uncertain, no other fish has a pedigree dating back for over 1,000 years.

Chinese books contain an assortment of references to red or golden fish from the beginning of time, but true authentication of the existence of the goldfish appears during the Sung Dynasty (960-1279 A.D.). After this period, there are increasing references to the goldfish in Chinese literature, the origins of its popularity as a pet. During the eleventh century, goldfish breeders were improving their stock and able to produce the gold colour with which we are familiar.

THE WORLDWIDE SPREAD OF GOLDFISH

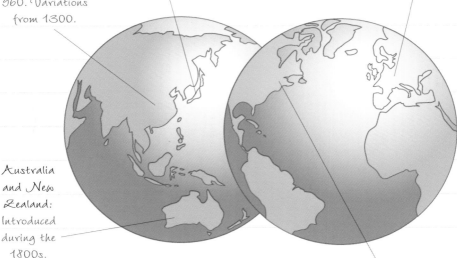

Europe: Introduced during the 1700s. Many fancy types did not appear until the 1900s.

Japan: Introduced in 1500. Breeding established by 1700 and some fancy forms developed.

China: Colour forms as pets by 960. Variations from 1300.

Australia and New Zealand: Introduced during the 1800s.

North America: introduced during the mid 1800s. A goldfish farm was established in Maryland by the late 1800s.

* In thirteenth-century China, goldfish were kept in ceramic bowls that were highly decorated outside, but plain white inside so that their aristocratic owners could view them from above.

▲ *Because goldfish are easy to keep in a compact aquarium, they are popular pets around the world.*

FANCY GOLDFISH

In 1200, we find the first reference to fancy goldfish – fish with snow-white, lustrous bodies and black spots called 'tortoiseshell fish'. After this, there is no further reference to fancy goldfish until the latter part of the Ming Dynasty (1368-1644), when a large number of multicoloured varieties are mentioned.

The development of fancy varieties of goldfish continued with the Egg fish, Fantails and Ryukin (the latter gave rise to the Veiltail) that appeared in the sixteenth century. By the seventeenth century, a whole range of goldfish of different colours and 'designs' was being bred in quantity.

TAIL VARIATIONS

Common
A single tail fin, with both lobes equal in both size and shape.

Comet
A single tail fin as in common goldfish, but both lobes are much larger.

Fantail
A twin tail that is divided and forked, united at the base with stiff rays.

Ranchu
A twin tail as in Fantail, but short and held at an elegant angle.

Oranda
A twin divided tail with weaker rays that allow the lobes to droop in a flowing manner.

* From ancient China to the present day, specialist breeders have passed on their secrets to succeeding generations.

THE HISTORY OF GOLDFISH

The goldfish hobby

Goldfish in the aquarium may well include the fancy varieties, such as the Veiltail, Oranda, Moor, Fantail, Pearlscale and Lionhead. For dedicated hobbyists, the list of varieties is much greater, although many will restrict their interest to just one or two. Nevertheless, many goldfish hobbyists are probably just as interested in good-quality Common goldfish, Shubunkins and Comets as they are in the more 'specialist' varieties.

Traditionally, China and Japan have been the source of common and fancy varieties of goldfish, although Italy, America and Israel produce large numbers of Common goldfish using intensive aquaculture techniques.

▲ *Goldfish are treasured pets for children as well as adults and may trigger a lifelong interest in fishkeeping as a hobby.*

DELICATE GOLDFISH VARIETIES

If you intend designing and installing an ornamental aquarium using plants, gravel and ornaments, you can consider keeping virtually any goldfish, with the exception of the Bubble-eye, Celestial and the Pompon. This is because in the case of the Bubble-eye, with its large sacks of water below its upward-looking eyes, there is a risk of the bubbles becoming caught up in the plants and decor or rupturing on sharp objects, such as the gravel. This would cause a fish great distress and could even result in death. Similar problems can occur with the Pompon, whose large narial pompons, or bouquets, can become caught up in plant growth. The Celestial, with its upward-facing eyes, faces an arduous existence for a different reason; as it swims around the aquarium, it is in danger of constantly knocking into objects that it simply cannot see. These fish are therefore best kept in a bare tank.

Bubble-eyes need extra care.

COMPATIBILITY

A factor to consider when keeping singletailed and twintailed goldfishes is the difference in their speed of movement. Singletails are faster and more active and this could become a stressful and damaging situation for the twintails in the competition for food and territory.

Think carefully about the type of food you offer to fishes with upward-looking eyes, such as Bubble-eyes and Celestials. They are going to have difficulty finding and picking up food that lies on the bottom of the tank.

As a rule of thumb, the safest strategy is to keep 'like with like'. This means you can keep any of the singletailed varieties together, plus the Jikin (an active twintailed variety similar to a Common goldfish but with a short, stubby divided tail). Alternatively, you can keep any of the round-bodied, twintail varieties together, other than Bubble-eyes, Celestials and Pompons, so that these fishes avoid being damaged either by other fishes or their environment.

▶ *Fast-moving varieties such as Comets are not the best tank companions for slower fancy goldfishes.*

KEEPING IN TOUCH

One way of becoming more involved with the hobby is to join one of the many societies. The benefits of joining include access to a wealth of information about keeping and breeding goldfish, accessing up-to-date information on new varieties and their availability, and showing fish. With the advent of the Internet, many goldfish societies throughout the world have created web pages and it is becoming much easier to locate and join them.

▶ *By using email and accessing the Internet, you can keep in touch with goldfish hobbyists around the world.*

The goldfish hobby

Successfully rearing goldfish to produce high-quality specimens with the desirable attributes for the particular variety takes dedication and patience. For serious breeders, the mark of success lies in showing fancy goldfish. Shows are not only attended by people who breed goldfish, but also by hobbyists who have acquired good-quality specimens and wish to exhibit them. The shows give them a chance to demonstrate their ability to manage and maintain the fish.

▲ For some hobbyists, exhibiting goldfish in competitive shows is a consuming passion, but it takes time to breed the best specimens.

SHOW STANDARDS

All varieties are judged by set standards in five categories: body, fins, colour, special characteristics, and condition and deportment. Each category can earn 20 points, with a possible total of 100, but with marks deducted for faults.

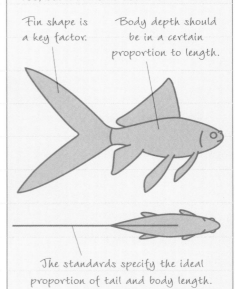

Fin shape is a key factor.

Body depth should be in a certain proportion to length.

The standards specify the ideal proportion of tail and body length.

◀ These are fishes in their show tanks after judging. The labels on the tanks indicate the position achieved and points scored. When the judging is over, exhibitors and the public are allowed into the hall.

JUDGING A RED METALLIC RANCHU (TOTAL SCORE: 76 POINTS)

Body (20 points)	Possible	Actual
Depth & length	6	5
Dorsal contour	5	4
Ventral contour	3	1.5
Lateral contour	3	3
Eyes & mouth	3	3
	20	**16.5**

Special characteristics (20 points)

The special characteristic of this variety is the development of the wen (hood) in three main areas:

	Possible	Actual
Cranial region	10	8
Infra-orbital region	5	3.5
Opercular region	5	4
	20	**15.5**

Colour (20 points)

The red of this fish is not of the highest intensity and does not extend into the fins.
Score: **13**

Fins (20 points)

Assuming the fish has twin anal fins and a divided caudal, all the other fins are good but not perfect.
Score: **16**

Condition and deportment (20 points)

The deportment has been marked low because of a tendency to hang head down.

	Possible	Actual
Condition	10	9
Deportment	10	6
	20	**15**

Popular varieties

The wide choice of goldfish varieties appeals to a range of hobbyists. Probably most people are familiar with the variations in the shape of the tail fin. which may be used to differentiate between varieties and place them into categories such as singletails, twintails and other varieties. The most obvious singletailed variety is the Common goldfish. Twintail goldfish are further subdivided into long- or veiltailed, and short- or fantailed varieties. Colour and patterns vary among goldfish.

▼ **Common goldfish**

Typically 'carp-shaped' fish, with paired pectoral and pelvic fins and single dorsal, anal and caudal fins. Colours include: metallic red, orange, yellow, white, red/orange- and-white, and red-and-black.

▼ **Oranda**

A short-bodied, high-backed fish with long, paired fins, a high dorsal fin and a hood growth covering the head. Some variants have telescope eyes.

▲ **Fantail**

A deep-bodied fish with a divided and forked tail fin. Bred in a range of colours, including metallic self, variegated and calico.

◄ **Shubunkin**

Basically a common goldfish with calico colours. The London Shubunkin (here) has a short rounded tail; the Bristol, longer fins all round.

◀ Panda Butterfly

A black-and-silver, fantail-type fish with divided tail that resembles a butterfly. Globe eyes as found in Moor and some other varieties.

▼ Pompon

The septum dividing each nostril develops into a fleshy lobe that resembles a pompon. Body shape as for the Bubble-eye. Solid and calico colours.

▼ Ranchu

Short, deep body, with a smoothly arched back and no dorsal fin. Hood may cover top of head or completely encase the head. Similar to Lionhead.

▶ Bubble-eye

Fluid-filled sacs beneath the eyes and a smoothly contoured body without a dorsal fin. Eyes are directed upwards, but do not bulge as in Celestials.

The tail should be divided and forked.

Colour and scales

COLOUR AND SCALES

The outermost layer of the skin – the epidermis – is a living tissue that forms a very fine coating over the scales. Immediately beneath these is the dermis, where the cells responsible for producing colour are found. 'True' colours are formed by chromatophores: erythrophores (orange and red); xanthophores (yellow); melanophores (black); and leucophores (white/silver).

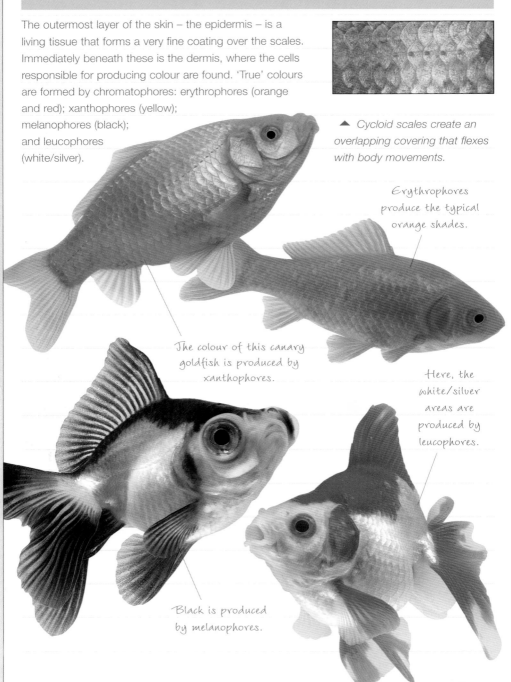

▲ *Cycloid scales create an overlapping covering that flexes with body movements.*

Erythrophores produce the typical orange shades.

The colour of this canary goldfish is produced by xanthophores.

Here, the white/silver areas are produced by leucophores.

Black is produced by melanophores.

REFLECTIVE VARIATIONS IN GOLDFISH

The shimmering appearance of a goldfish is produced by reflective guanine, a waste product. The angle of light affects the degree and coloration of the metallic effect.

Scale | Reflective guanine on scales and in dermis.

▲ Metallic scales. Layers of iridocytes (guanine crystals) beneath each scale and in the dermis itself give the goldfish its characteristic metallic sheen by reflecting light falling on the skin.

Guanine layer only in dermis.

▲ Nacreous scales. Here, iridocytes are just present in the dermis and can only shine through a limited amount, giving a 'mother of pearl' appearance.

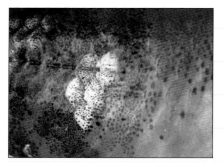

No reflective guanine on scales or in dermis.

▲ Matt scales. With no iridocytes beneath the scales or in the dermis, the scales appear translucent and the coloration is provided by pigment cells alone.

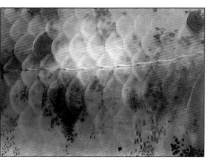

◀ The virtual colours on a CD are caused by light dispersal and diffraction in the same way as iridocytes create colour and sheen under the skin of goldfishes.

COLOUR AND SCALES

How goldfish swim

The Common goldfish is a 'typical' fish in terms of its body shape, internal organs and complement of fins. The tail and the muscular rear part of the body – the caudal peduncle – provide forward thrust by sweeping from side to side. The other fins act as stabilisers, steering paddles and brakes. The swimbladder enables the fish to hang motionless at a particular depth and then use the pectoral fins near the gill covers to make small changes in position and direction, including swimming backwards.

▼ *A front view clearly shows how the fins are used to steer the fish.*

Caudal fin or tail.

Dorsal fin

Anal fin.

Pelvic fin (paired).

Pectoral fins

Pectoral fin being flared as a 'brake'.

* *The dorsal fin acts as the main keel to stop the fish rolling over as it swims along.*

▲ *All the fins are at work here as the fish turns and changes its position in the water.*

HOW THE SWIMBLADDER WORKS

The swimbladder is a gas-filled bag in the centre of the body that acts as a buoyancy device. In goldfishes, gas can be added or withdrawn from the swimbladder to allow the fish to remain buoyant at any depth.

▶ *Some varieties (here Hama Nishiki) may have swimbladder problems because of their shape.*

The gas inside is mainly oxygen and can be used for respiration in extreme circumstances.

The pneumatic duct allows the fish to top up the swimbladder with air.

Gas glands on the inner surface release or absorb gas as the fish goes up or down in the water.

Intestine

Air gulped at the surface passes down the back of the throat into the pneumatic duct.

▼ *When swimming forward, the tail provides momentum and the other fins are tucked away.*

The dorsal is swept back.

Large caudal fin of a Comet goldfish providing forward thrust.

Vital systems

Like all fish, goldfish extract oxygen from the water through their gills and release waste carbon dioxide into the expelled flow. They have a simple heart that pumps blood around the body through a network of arteries and veins. Their adaptation to life in freshwater includes an ability to produce dilute urine to carry away toxic waste products, which also diffuse out of the gills.

HOW THE GILLS WORK

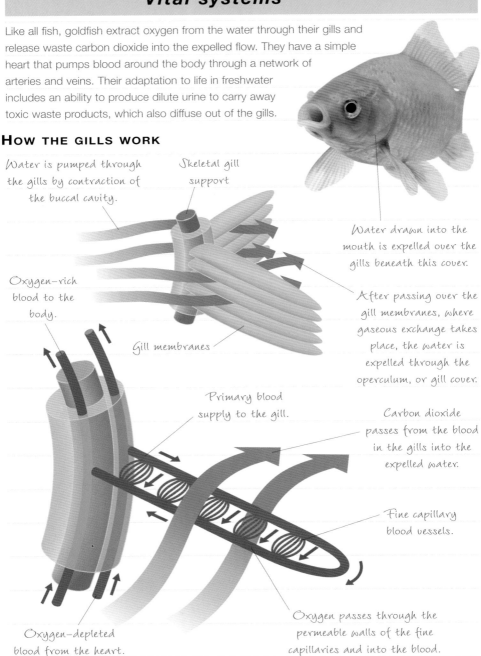

Water is pumped through the gills by contraction of the buccal cavity.

Skeletal gill support

Oxygen-rich blood to the body.

Gill membranes

Water drawn into the mouth is expelled over the gills beneath this cover.

After passing over the gill membranes, where gaseous exchange takes place, the water is expelled through the operculum, or gill cover.

Primary blood supply to the gill.

Carbon dioxide passes from the blood in the gills into the expelled water.

Fine capillary blood vessels.

Oxygen-depleted blood from the heart.

Oxygen passes through the permeable walls of the fine capillaries and into the blood.

VITAL SYSTEMS

BLOOD CIRCULATION

Oxygenated blood delivers oxygen to the tissues and carries away waste products.

Blood passing through the gills takes up oxygen and loses carbon dioxide.

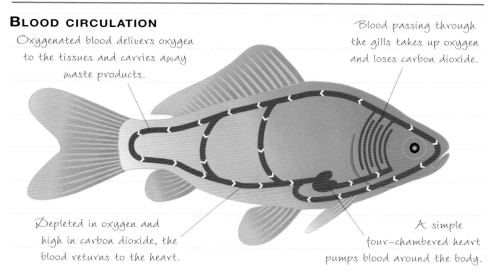

Depleted in oxygen and high in carbon dioxide, the blood returns to the heart.

A simple four-chambered heart pumps blood around the body.

WATER REGULATION IN GOLDFISH

Salts

Water

The kidneys retain body salts but remove excess water.

Water and salts are absorbed through the permeable membranes of the gills.

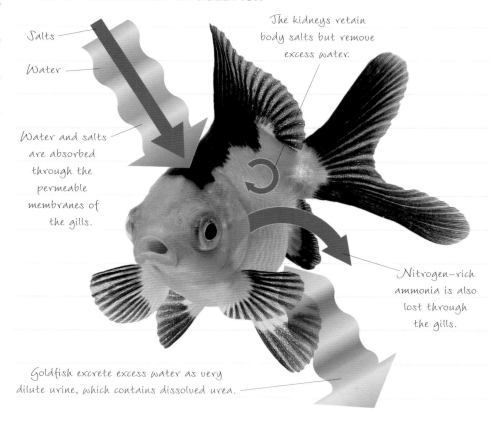

Nitrogen-rich ammonia is also lost through the gills.

Goldfish excrete excess water as very dilute urine, which contains dissolved urea.

Sensory systems

Goldfish are acutely aware of the world around them. Water is an excellent medium to transmit sound (as vibrations), pressure waves and dissolved substances that can be smelt or tasted. Goldfish do not have external ears, but their internal ear canals can translate underwater vibrations into clear sound. Much fainter pressure waves can be picked up by the lateral line system that connects to a series of pits along the flanks. Goldfish have twin nostrils and a well-developed sense of smell.

HOW GOLDFISH HEAR

Sound travels as a series of vibrations.

The vibrations generate nerve impulses in the inner ear that are carried to the brain and heard as sounds.

Linking bones transfer the vibrations to the inner ear.

The swimbladder picks up and amplifies the sound vibrations.

THE SENSE OF SMELL

Muscular contractions may help the water to flow through.

Flaps guide the water in and out.

Water flows into the nostril as the fish swims along.

Receptor cells respond to substances dissolved in the water and generate nerve impulses interpreted by the brain as smell.

THE PRESSURE-SENSITIVE LATERAL LINE

▶ *Look closely at the flanks of a goldfish and you will see a line of pores running from head to tail. These are the openings to the lateral line system.*

* *The lateral line allows fish to 'map out' what's happening in their immediate surroundings.*

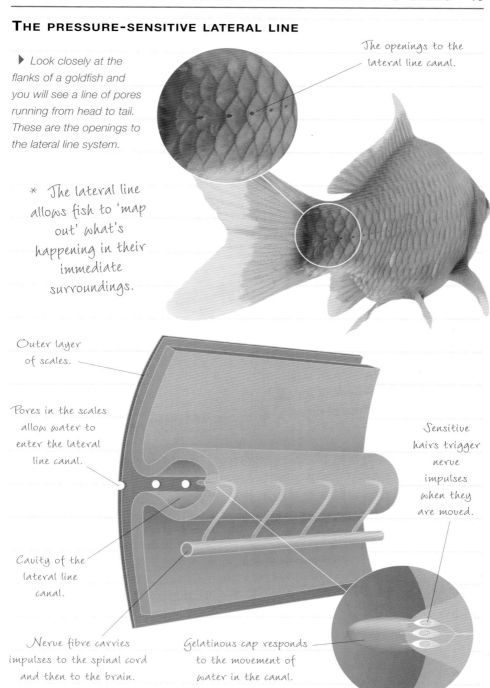

The openings to the lateral line canal.

Outer layer of scales.

Pores in the scales allow water to enter the lateral line canal.

Sensitive hairs trigger nerve impulses when they are moved.

Cavity of the lateral line canal.

Nerve fibre carries impulses to the spinal cord and then to the brain.

Gelatinous cap responds to the movement of water in the canal.

Bowl or aquarium?

Most of us have always associated keeping goldfish in bowls. Old-fashioned goldfish bowls had a very narrow neck, which prevented the water from absorbing sufficient oxygen. In addition to the problems of low dissolved oxygen, these early bowls were poorly filtered and really did not benefit the welfare of the goldfish. The traditional rectangular aquarium could be both aerated and filtered, even if the overall volume of water was similar to that of the goldfish bowl.

Improvements in aquarium technology have addressed the problems of aerating and filtering a goldfish bowl, so these are now quite suitable for keeping goldfish. The choice now is purely personal preference.

▶ *This modern goldfish bowl has a capacity of 30 litres (6.6 gallons).*

▼ *An electric pump draws water down through the substrate and upwards via a simple sponge filter.*

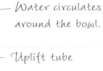

Water circulates around the bowl.

Uplift tube

Sponge filter

Coarse ceramic substrate acts as a biological filter.

* *Today it is much easier to provide the ideal living conditions for your goldfish in either a bowl or aquarium.*

▲ A compact rectangular aquarium complete with real and plastic plants.

Fluorescent tube provides light for fish and plants.

▼ The life-support systems that sustain the plants and fish.

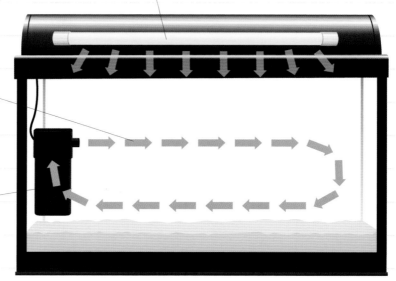

Filtered water is pumped across the aquarium.

Internal power filter draws water in near the bottom of the tank.

BOWL OR AQUARIUM?

Setting up an aquarium – location

The best way to keep many of the fancy varieties of goldfish is in an aquarium, and you can choose from a range of different sizes. Aim for a minimum tank size of 60x30x30cm (24x12x12in), although it is better to select the largest aquarium you can afford and accommodate; goldfish thrive where they have plenty of space. It is also best best to invest in a purpose-built stand or cabinet.

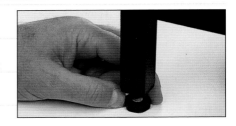

▲ *Adjust the screw feet on each leg of the stand to ensure that everything is level.*

WHERE TO SITE THE TANK

Good position: *Even if the aquarium is next to a chimney, the amount of heat that penetrates is insignificant.*

Good position: *A quiet alcove with access to service the tank and to electricity.*

Bad position: *Risk of draughts and disturbance from people passing by.*

Good position: *The tank will not be affected by people passing by.*

Bad position: *Cooking fumes in the kitchen may affect the fish.*

Bad position: *The fish will be disturbed by the sound and vibration of the door closing.*

Good position: *A dark, quiet corner can be enhanced by an attractive aquarium.*

Bad position: *In a bright conservatory there is too much light on the tank. It will get too hot by day and cold at night.*

Hallway

Living room

Kitchen

Dining room

Conservatory

SIZES AND CAPACITIES OF STANDARD TANKS

TANK (HEIGHT/WIDTH/DEPTH)	VOLUME	WEIGHT OF WATER
60x30x30cm (24x12x12in)	55 litres (12 gallons)	55kg (120lb)
60x30x38cm (24x12x15in)	68 litres (15 gallons)	68kg (150lb)
90x30x30cm (36x12x12in)	82 litres (18 gallons)	82kg (180lb)
90x30x38cm (36x12x15in)	104 litres (23 gallons)	104kg (230lb)
120x30x30cm (48x12x12in)	109 litres (24 gallons)	109kg (240lb)
120x30x38cm (48x12x15in)	136 litres (30 gallons)	136kg (300lb)

▶ *A custom-built hood with an integral light fitting and a condensation tray to protect the light tube from splashes. The starter unit is concealed behind a separate panel.*

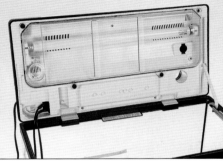

A black baseboard makes a useful shelf.

▲ *Metal stands are supplied flat-packed.*

FISH TANKS AND CHILDREN

The height of the tank from the floor is an important consideration, especially if there are young children who might run their wheeled toys into it. Stands and cabinets raise the tank to a good viewing height, but if you consider placing another aquarium on the lower level of one of the stands, be sure the location is childproof. This is as much for the safety of the child – who might inadvertently crack the tank – as the fish, should the child be 'helpful' and feed them (usually with a complete pot of food!) or, at worst, put undesirable substances into the aquarium.

SETTING UP AN AQUARIUM

Setting up an aquarium – substrates

The aquarium featured in this setting up sequence measures 60x30x38cm (24x12x15in) and once filled will contain about 68 litres (15 gallons) of water, weighing 68kg (150lb). The floor must be able to support this considerable weight, particularly if the aquarium is sited in an upstairs room. If in any doubt, consult a structural engineer. Once you have placed the tank on a stand or cabinet and made it level, clean the glass inside and out. The next task is to add a layer of substrate. Although sold as 'washed', aquarium gravel still contains dust that you must first flush away. Wash the gravel in several changes of clean water until it runs clear. The ideal depth should be 7.5cm (3in), which would support the roots of suitable aquarium plants.

CLEANING AND LEVELLING THE TANK

▲ During storage, new tanks accumulate fine dust that will leave a film on the water surface when the tank is filled. Use water and a clean cloth to clean the inside of the glass.

▲ It is safe to use a non-abrasive spray cleaner on the outside glass. On tanks that have been shrink-wrapped or banded with tape there may be sticky residues to remove.

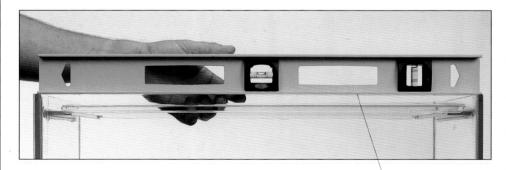

▲ Use a spirit level from side to side and back to front to ensure that the stand is true. Test it again when the tank is in its final position. Mistakes are difficult to rectify later on.

If necessary, lay the spirit level on a flat board.

AQUARIUM SUBSTRATES

Polished pebbles are decorative but uneaten food can lodge between the grains.

Black gravel shows off the colour of the fishes.

Choose non-toxic coloured gravels.

River sand does not damage the barbels of bottom-living fish, nor does it compact down.

Coarse   Medium   Fine

▲ *Coarse, medium and fine gravel make ideal substrates for all sizes of aquarium.*

▲ *Add the substrate in manageable handfuls or use a jug. Do not drop it in from a height.*

CHOOSING SUBSTRATES

When choosing substrates, always consider the needs of the fishes and whether the substrate is going to act as a plant-growing medium. Fish do not like substrates that are too pale. They reflect overhead light and make the tank occupants feel insecure. Dark material shows off their colours better. For a natural effect, slope the gravel slightly from front to back. Substrates should be inert, which means that they should not alter the chemical composition of the water. Always ask for lime-free gravel, and look out for any white fragments of calcareous material, such as shells, that could make the water too alkaline. Do not collect your own gravel from river beds or beaches, as you may be disturbing natural spawning sites and shelter for fish fry.

SETTING UP AN AQUARIUM

Setting up an aquarium – filtration

An external power filter saves precious space within a relatively small aquarium, while offering a large volume of media to deal with the considerable waste generated by goldfish. It is relatively bulky, but can be kept on the shelf below the tank or inside a cabinet cupboard.

Filter wool sandwiches activated carbon.

Carbon can be kept in a bag.

Use only branded aquarium filter wool.

Pelleted biomedia support good bacteria.

A coarse foam pad traps large dirt particles.

▲ *An external power filter works by drawing water through the various media and pumping it back into the aquarium. It accommodates more media for bacteria to colonise.*

▲ *Position the intake pipe (left) and the return pipe at the rear of the tank at opposite ends to create a good flow.*

▲ *Pour the activated carbon into a bag formed from a stocking or pair of tights and tie a loose knot.*

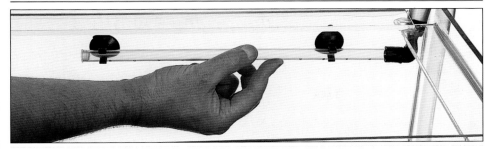

▲ A spraybar attached to the back glass is an alternative way of returning water from the power filter. The holes can be positioned to the rear to reduce turbulence.

▶ Position the return jet so that the flow is at, just above or just below the water surface. Cut the inlet and return pipes to a suitable length to keep them tidy.

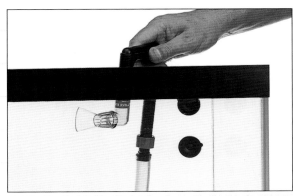

▲ Pass the intake pipe through the aperture at the rear corner of the tank.

Leave a free flow of air around the filter.

▲ To deliver aerated water back to the tank, use a multi-directional jet.

◀ External filters are easy to access for maintenance.

Setting up an aquarium – heating

A heater in a coldwater tank is not the contradiction it might appear. Although goldfish do not need the degree of warmth required by tropical fishes, a stable temperature is still essential to their well-being. This is usually provided in a centrally heated house during the day, but at night the domestic thermostat is often turned down, leading to a distinct fluctuation in the aquarium temperature over a 24-hour period. This is not good for your fishes or any natural plants in the aquarium. With a heater installed you have more control over the aquatic environment; a 100watt model will be quite adequate for a 60cm (24in) tank. Always install the unit at an angle, so that the rising heat does not directly pass the thermostat. The sensor should sample the ambient tank temperature, not a localised hotspot.

Digital thermometers stuck to the outside glass are popular.

The in-tank alcohol thermometer is held in place with suckers.

* *Never turn on the heater unless the tank is filled and the water level reaches the minimum specified on the unit.*

Leave a gap between the bottom of the heater and the substrate.

▲ *Combined electronic heater/thermostats are housed inside the tank.*

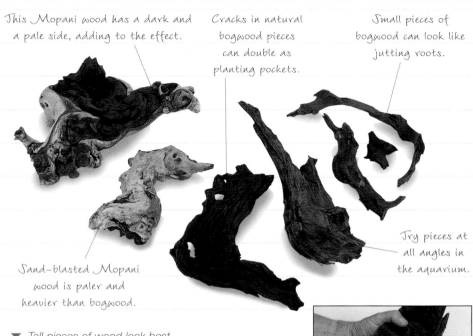

This Mopani wood has a dark and a pale side, adding to the effect.

Cracks in natural bogwood pieces can double as planting pockets.

Small pieces of bogwood can look like jutting roots.

Sand–blasted Mopani wood is paler and heavier than bogwood.

Try pieces at all angles in the aquarium.

▼ Tall pieces of wood look best at the rear and sides of the tank.

▶ Before adding it to the tank, clean shop-bought wood with a stiff brush and warm water to remove dust.

Do not allow any decor to touch the heater or filter equipment.

SETTING UP AN AQUARIUM

Setting up an aquarium – rocks

With any pieces of bogwood in place, now is the time to add some rocks. Aquarium retailers offer a wide choice of decorative rocks for aquarium use. The smooth contours of waterworn rocks look the most natural, with no sharp edges to injure fish. As with the gravel, make sure each rock is clean by washing it thoroughly in warm water. Place rocks carefully in the tank, starting with the largest pieces.

Use slate to shield the sides of the tank and give fish a sense of security.

Westmorland rock is fairly inert unless the water is very acidic.

Do not collect pebbles and boulders from the wild. Most aquatic shops stock them.

Chunks of lava rock, although artificial, are not moulded but come in random shapes and sizes.

Scattered slate pebbles create the illusion of a weathered rock face.

Sandstone chunks have a warm brown colour, but some types are too soft for aquarium use.

▶ Group larger rocks towards the back and sides of the tank. Odd-numbered groups (three, five, seven, etc.) are visually more pleasing than even numbers.

Grotto ceramic, an inert manmade rock, supports bacteria in its porous structure.

Coloured rocks can be dramatic. Check that they are safe to use in the aquarium.

▲ If a rock fizzes when vinegar is dripped onto it, this shows that it is calcareous and may affect water chemistry.

Granite is safe, but rather stark and angular when broken into small pieces.

This red, striated piece of rock is sold as 'African rock'.

Hand-carved 'rainbow rock'.

Test this 'ocean rock' before use.

Hard coal looks good with black gravel. Scrub it first to remove any dust.

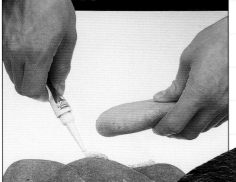

▲ To avoid rock falls, secure pieces with silicone squeezed onto clean surfaces. Trim any excess once dry.

SETTING UP AN AQUARIUM

Setting up an aquarium – adding water

At this stage, add water to the tank. Goldfish are adaptable to variations in water chemistry and tolerant of a wide range of pH and hardness values. Use your local tapwater, but either allow it to stand for 24 hours in a clean container to dissipate the chlorine (ideally with an airstone bubbling) or use a water conditioner to make it suitable for use. Do not use rainwater because it may contain pollutants. Distilled or purified water may seem ideal, but they are lacking any minerals and are not suitable for aquarium use.

◀ *Dechlorinators that remove chlorine and chloramine from tapwater are widely available and effective. Follow the instructions supplied.*

You can check the pH reading of your water using a test kit. Follow the directions.

▼ *Start by pouring water from a clean jug onto a flat rock or a saucer to avoid disturbing the substrate.*

Fill the tank to 10cm (4in) below the final level.

THE NITROGEN CYCLE

When you add fish to an aquarium, they will produce nitrogenous waste, largely in the form of ammonia. This is the starting point for the nitrogen cycle, a natural process involving beneficial bacteria that convert toxic wastes to less harmful substances. The biological medium in the filter system support these bacteria and help to keep the water clean. Once fish are added, the first three weeks or so are critical for a new aquarium. This is because the bacteria need time to grow in the filter media so that they can process the waste efficiently.

Plants use ammonia and nitrates as a food source and incorporate the nitrogen into proteins that are in turn eaten by fish and other creatures.

Fish consume plants and other nitrogen–containing foods and excrete nitrogenous waste.

Ammonia, NH_3, is the main waste product and is excreted from the gills and in lower concentrations in the urine.

Bacteria living in the substrate convert toxic ammonia to nitrite, NO_2, still poisonous to fish.

Different bacteria 'feed' on nitrite and produce nitrate, NO_3, a much less harmful substance.

Setting up an aquarium – decor

Goldfishes like to dig around or snack on real plants, so artificial plants are ideal. Plastic plants are inert and virtually everlasting. They provide shelter and a spawning medium for fish, and their leaves and stems will be colonised by the same bacteria that live in the filter. However, because they do not take up nitrates, as real plants do, you must pay extra attention to water changes. When they first go into the aquarium, even the most realistic replicas can look 'too good to be true', but as the leaves acquire a fine algae coating, the colours will tone down.

▲ Add or remove sections to vary the height of plastic plants, leaving a 'growing tip' in place for realism.

▼ Slide the holdfast at the base of the plastic plant sideways into the substrate.

Cabomba

Hygrophila

Vallisneria

Limnophila aquatica

Ceratopsis cornuta

Myriophyllum

* Enhance the effect by mixing different sizes of the same plant.

Other decorative items

Glass decor can look very attractive when the lights shines through it.

Bamboo canes suit a coldwater tank.

Well-washed bottles suggest the bottom of a river or canal through which boats passed long ago!

* Air-operated ornaments help to agitate the water surface and provide movement.

Small shy fishes will welcome these refuges.

An air-operated diver is functional and fun.

Make sure that sunken galleons and similar items are safe for the aquarium.

Very young children delight in colourful, cartoonlike ornaments such as these.

Setting up an aquarium – plants

A goldfish aquarium in a centrally heated room rarely falls below 18°C (64°F) and will support many plant species sold for tropical aquariums. The plants featured on these pages are undemanding and easy to replace if nibbled. Choose healthy plants with strong root systems that will establish in the substrate.

▲ These goldfish are at home among the fine leaves of Elodea canadensis.

Vallisneria spiralis (straight vallis) is ideal for the background.

Pinching out the tips of myriophyllum keeps the plant compact.

This plant will grow well in good light.

The leathery leaves grow in flat rosettes.

Cryptocoryne willisii may reach no more than 4–5cm (1.6–2in) in the aquarium.

* Always buy true aquatic plants, not houseplants that will live for only a few weeks before rotting away.

Hygrophila polysperma is readily propagated by top cuttings.

▲ *Bacopa caroliniana is ideal for the hard-water environment of a typical coldwater setup. It does best in clean, clear water.*

Setting up an aquarium – plants

When building up a planted display, use larger plants at the back and sides of the tank to create a framework. Turn each plant until you find its most pleasing 'face'. Gently hold the plant near the base and, using a finger of the same hand, make a hold in the substrate. Slide the plant into the hole, just deep enough to prevent it coming loose. Continue planting towards the front, using smaller species to allow swimming room for the fish.

▶ *Lobelia cardinalis has dark green to reddish leaves and responds to trimming back.*

◀ *Sagittaria pusilla will tolerate hard water and survives in moderate to low light.*

* It is often easier and more effective to use a limited number of plant species in larger groupings.

▶ *This is just one of several Ludwigia species suitable for a coldwater tank.*

▲ *Flexible Hydrocotyle (pennywort) stems sway with the water current.*

▶ *Ceratophyllum demersum provides cover and spawning sites for fish.*

SETTING UP AN AQUARIUM

▶ *The whorls of Cabomba create attractive patterns under the tank lights.*

Keep the finely branched leaves free of debris.

Setting up an aquarium – lighting

Adding a lighting system to the tank enables you to view the fish and provides vital illumination for real plants to flourish. Fluorescent tubes are the most popular form of aquarium lighting. You can fit them yourself, as shown here, or you can buy custom-built hoods with integrated light fittings. Tubes are very efficient, use little electricity and relatively cheap when used in small numbers. It is best to change them every year to maintain good lighting levels in the aquarium.

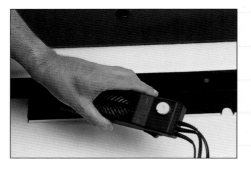

1 Position the starter unit on the shelf at the rear of the hood, where it will be more stable. Make sure it is not plugged into the electricity supply.

2 Feed the flying leads through the holes on either side of the shelf. Each endcap has two holes corresponding to the pins on the tube.

3 Line up the pins on the tube with the holes in the endcaps and push home firmly. Plastic collars around the caps ensure they make a watertight connection.

Handle fluorescent tubes with care to avoid breakage.

4 Fit the clips into the hood, using either the plastic nuts and bolts or self-tapping assemblies supplied with the lighting kit.

5 Align the tube centrally and gently push it into the retaining clips. Plug in and switch on the unit to test that everything is working correctly.

TUBE COLOURS

Fluorescent tubes are available in a range of 'colours'. Altering the chemical coating on the inside of the tube changes the spectrum of light it produces. Pink/purple tubes produce light that helps plants to flourish but gives the tank an eerie glow. Combining this with a full-spectrum white tube, particularly a triphosphor type, provides a balanced output that suits most aquariums.

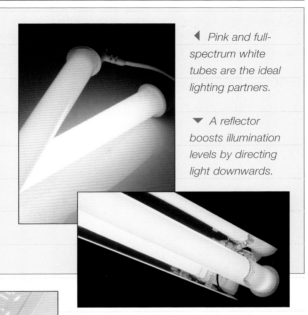

◀ *Pink and full-spectrum white tubes are the ideal lighting partners.*

▼ *A reflector boosts illumination levels by directing light downwards.*

6 Flexible condensation trays are easy to trim with scissors. Cut the rear corners to fit filter tubes and heater cables.

7 Fit the modified tray over the glass ledges around the top of the tank. You may need to trim one or more edges so that it fits snugly without any buckling.

8 Position the completed hood on top of the aquarium. Make sure that it fits flush and does not trap any pipes or cables.

Setting up an aquarium – backgrounds

The finishing touch is to add a background to the tank. Fitting a decorative plastic background to the outside of the back glass conceals any electric cables, filter pipework and the wall behind, adding to the overall visual appeal of the aquarium display. Backgrounds are sold off the roll or to an approximate size, and are easy to trim with scissors. The design is a matter of personal taste: a planted underwater scene, tree roots, rockwork or classical temples are all popular.

You can also buy a range of solid textured panels for the back of tank, but these should go inside right at the start.

Cork tiles stuck to the outside glass create a good neutral effect.

▲ *Stretch the background tightly across the outside back glass and secure with strips of adhesive tape. Make sure the glass is dry to help adhesion.*

Plain black is a safe choice that will make any tank look good. Blue on the reverse can make a tank look cold.

A design with rocks and plants is fine, as long as your aquarium display features these elements, too.

Classical temples ruins could form a credible background if your tank ornaments are in the same style.

This rock design gives a realistic 3D effect and can be trimmed top or bottom without spoiling the result.

MATURING THE TANK

With the tank complete, the great temptation is to add fish. Resist it! Self-restraint is needed while the filtration system matures biologically, which will take up to six weeks. If you have real plants, these will need to establish their root systems without disruption. Leave the lights on for 10-14 hours a day to promote growth. After two weeks, carry out a nitrite test and if the reading is acceptable, you can add your first fish. Test for nitrite daily and if necessary make a partial water change. Add the remaining fish gradually over the coming weeks.

▼ *The completed tank needs time to mature. You can add a proprietary bacterial culture to 'seed' the filter, but take things slowly.*

▼ *Now you can fit a thermometer. This internal type is fixed with a single sucker. Attach it in a top corner away from the filter outflow.*

SETTING UP AN AQUARIUM

Setting up an aquarium – buying fish

Before buying goldfish, tour your local aquatic dealers and find one prepared to spend time to help you. Better still, take along an experienced hobbyist friend, as they will know what to look out for. The shop could be an independent retailer, part of a chain or a franchise attached to a garden centre – it does not matter, as long as the staff are knowledgeable and the fishes healthy. Later, you may wish to specialise in more exotic fancy goldfish, but at this stage fish health is more important than pedigree. Try to visit aquatic shops midweek when business is fairly quiet and the staff will have more time to discuss your needs. Good dealers will be cruel to be kind, so do not be upset if they refuse to sell you the fishes on the same day as you buy the hardware. They will know that rushing things is the sure-fire route to early failure, and losing a potential lifelong customer makes bad business sense.

▼ *When buying goldfish, take your time to look at all the fish on offer before deciding on the ones you want for you aquarium.*

▲ *When you have made your choice, the dealer will use a large soft net to isolate the fish and then gently scoop it up in the hand and transfer it to a plastic bag that will be sealed with plenty of air or oxygen above the water.*

* Only buy a few fish at a time so that you can build up your stock gradually.

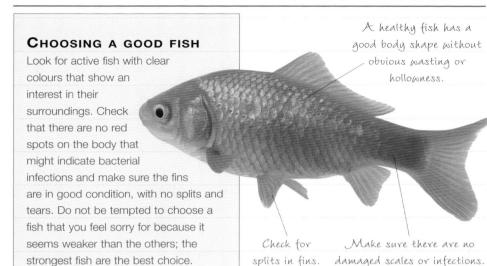

CHOOSING A GOOD FISH

Look for active fish with clear colours that show an interest in their surroundings. Check that there are no red spots on the body that might indicate bacterial infections and make sure the fins are in good condition, with no splits and tears. Do not be tempted to choose a fish that you feel sorry for because it seems weaker than the others; the strongest fish are the best choice.

A healthy fish has a good body shape without obvious wasting or hollowness.

Check for splits in fins.

Make sure there are no damaged scales or infections.

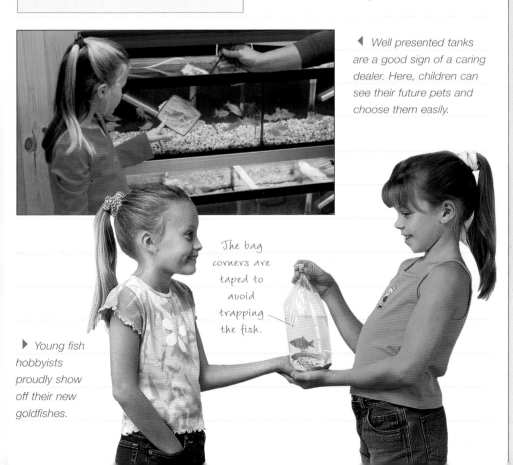

◀ *Well presented tanks are a good sign of a caring dealer. Here, children can see their future pets and choose them easily.*

The bag corners are taped to avoid trapping the fish.

▶ *Young fish hobbyists proudly show off their new goldfishes.*

SETTING UP AN AQUARIUM

Setting up an aquarium – adding fish

Take your time choosing your first fishes. They should be with you for quite some time, so buy specimens that appeal to you. Once the dealer has netted them into a plastic bag, hold them up and examine them from all angles to make sure they are healthy, with no split fins, deformities or ulcers. Pay special attention to the belly area, which is easy to overlook, but often the site of infection. The bag containing the fishes and a small amount of water is inflated with air or oxygen and sealed with a rubber band. Ask the dealer to tape up the corners so that small fishes cannot become trapped and damage themselves.

THE JOURNEY HOME

For the journey home, place the plastic bag into a brown paper outer or black bin liner to help keep the occupants calm. On long journeys, stand the bag upright inside an insulated polystyrene box. Hold it in place with balls of scrunched up newspaper. Go straight home; the less time the fish spend in transit, the better they will cope.

Keeping the fish in the dark helps them stay calm during the journey.

* After transferring fish, dispose of all plastic bags immediately.

1 Once home, gently remove the outer wrappings. If the trip has been short, float the sealed bag in the tank for 10 minutes to equalise the temperatures.

2 Following a longer journey, open up the top of the bag to dispel the stale air. Roll down the sides to form a collar. Leave the lights off, as they will only stress the fish. After a few minutes, check the water temperature by dipping a finger into the bag and then into the tank. You will be able to tell if the fishes are ready to be released into the aquarium.

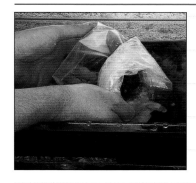

3 Be gentle when transferring the fishes from the bag to the tank. Turn the bag on its side and hold it open with one hand while you gently tip it with the other. Give the fish plenty of time to swim out. Make sure they all do, and that none is trapped in the rolled-down collar.

* If you lose a fish soon after stocking, do not panic, but try to pin down the cause.

THE COMPLETED DISPLAY

When all the fish are in the tank, carefully replace the condensation tray and hood and leave the fish to settle down for a further 30 minutes. You can then return to switch on the light and admire the finished aquarium.

Heavy early feeds will only overload the filtration, so wait until the following morning before adding a very small amount of flake or tablet food.

At first, the fish may hide among the plants or behind rocks and wood, but they will emerge when they have gained confidence.

In the early days, the fish may not be showing their best colours. This is normal following the stress of moving to a new home.

SETTING UP AN AQUARIUM

Routine maintenance

Regular maintenance is essential to keep your fish and plants healthy and your tank looking good. Most tasks take only a few minutes and should be seen as a pleasure, not a chore. Goldfishes generate a lot of solid waste that must not be allowed to build up on the floor of the tank or go into solution. Water changes are essential to dilute pollutants, particularly nitrates, and with a little practice you will be able to siphon out dirt at the same time as you carry out a partial water change. This is also the time to remove algae from the tank glass with a magnet or scraper and to tidy the plants. Remember to condition the new water that you add to the tank.

CLEANING AN INTERNAL FILTER

Turn off the electricity at the main supply. Leave the heater to cool down before lowering the water level.

1 Unplug and remove the filter and lift it into a bowl into which you have siphoned 2.5-5cm (1-2in) of tank water.

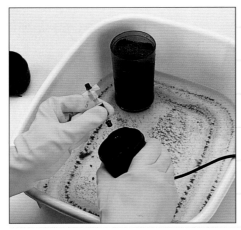

2 Remove the impeller and shaft and clean off the slime. Wipe inside the impeller housing with a clean, soft cloth.

3 Remove the sponge and rinse it in the aquarium water. This way you will not destroy the beneficial bacteria in the filter.

ROUTINE MAINTENANCE

REGULAR MAINTENANCE

DAILY

Remove uneaten food

Check the health of the fish

Check the water
temperature

Check equipment (filters,
lights, airpump)

WEEKLY/EVERY TWO WEEKS

Make a 10-20% partial
water change

Test for pH and nitrite level

Clean front glass of algae

Remove dead plant matter
and vacuum substrate
with a gravel cleaner

Clean cover glass or
condensation tray

MONTHLY/AS REQUIRED

Clean filter and replace
expendable media if
necessary

▶ *Testing the
water for nitrite
level is a vital
routine. This test
involves adding
a tablet to a
sample of tank
water in a tube,
and comparing
the colour change
to a printed chart.*

EVERY 6-12 MONTHS

Service airpump and
filter/powerhead motors

Replace lighting tubes

Replace airstones and
airline

Scrub rocks/bogwood and
plastic plants to remove
build-up of algae

MAKING A PARTIAL WATER CHANGE

Use a plain, light-coloured plastic
bucket (reserved for aquarium use)
to siphon the water into. The colour
of the water will clearly show up in
this. Stand the bucket on the floor,
place the gravel cleaner in the tank
and the free end of the tube in the
bucket. Start the siphoning action.
You can stop the water flow by
taking the gravel cleaner out of the
water. Avoid sucking up small fish or
bruising delicate plant leaves. Use
siphoned water to clean filters.

◀ *A gravel
cleaner works by
sucking up water
and whisking
away the debris.
With a siphonic
action cleaner,
you combine the
cleaning process
with a partial
water change.*

Routine maintenance

Biological filters should run 24 hours a day to support the colonies of beneficial (aerobic) bacteria that break down aquarium toxins into relatively harmless nitrate. The usual sign that a filter needs cleaning is a fall-off in flow rate, caused by partial blockage of the mechanical media inside. If you do not attend to this, water will take the easiest line of resistance and parts of the media will become deoxygenated and foul as good bacteria are replaced by anaerobic bugs. The result is a filter that smells of rotten eggs.

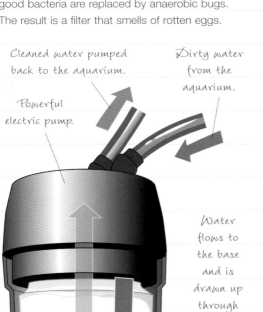

Cleaned water pumped back to the aquarium.

Dirty water from the aquarium.

Powerful electric pump.

Water flows to the base and is drawn up through the filter media.

Inside the canister filter media are arranged in layers.

1 Turn the coupling taps to the 'off' position and undo the plastic nuts securing the taps to the filter body. Place the filter in a shallow bowl and tilt it to drain off most of the water.

2 Remove the motor from the canister by releasing the locking tabs and separating the two main components. Remove the impeller and clean all plastic parts with a cloth.

ROUTINE MAINTENANCE

 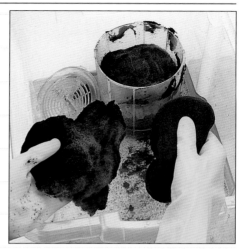

3 Remove the internal basket. Some filters have separate modules for different filter materials, but this is a one-piece assembly.

4 Remove the media from the internal basket. Discard the soiled filter floss and exhausted activated carbon.

THE CONDENSATION TRAY

Plastic condensation trays scratch easily, so use only a clean, damp cloth to wipe them. Replace trays the moment they start to become opaque, as salts and debris reduce the penetration of light into the aquarium.

5 Gently wash the permanent media, loose-fill an old stocking with fresh carbon and reassemble the media. Replace the motor unit. Couple the filter to the taps and turn them to the 'on' position.

Feeding goldfish

Captive fish are entirely dependent on their owner for food, which must be offered regularly and in a varied form to mimic as closely as possible what would be available in the wild. Goldfishes are omnivores, meaning they eat a variety of items including bacteria from the sediments, microscopic animals and plants, plus larger aquatic plants, insects and crustaceans. Captive goldfish should be given commercially manufactured foods that contain all the essential nutrients and vitamins to keep them fit and healthy.

THE BASIC DIET

Flake foods are probably the most common type of manufactured diet, but you can also buy pellets and foodsticks for larger fish. Always gauge the size of food you offer your stock on the basis of the smallest fish to ensure that they all get sufficient to eat. Fancy varieties of goldfish can suffer from buoyancy disorders, and floating foods, which are consumed at the water surface, may aggravate the condition.

▲ *Once fish are accustomed to you, they will take flakes from your fingers. Resist the temptation to overfeed.*

Freeze-dried bloodworm. These are also available in frozen form.

Affix stick-on tablets to the aquarium glass.

Sinking granules provide food at substrate level.

Freeze-dried tubifex cubes are safe for aquarium use.

Proprietary flake food can be crumbled to suit small goldfish.

▲ *Tubifex cubes stick to the tank glass and the fish cluster around as the cubes disintegrate.*

▼ *Aquarium goldfish should feed throughout the year as the water temperature will be fairly constant. Offer a varied diet.*

AQUARIUM FEEDING STRATEGY

In the aquarium, it is best to feed goldfish a pinch at a time, offering them as much as they will eat in two or three minutes on a daily basis. Initially, healthy goldfish are very keen to feed and will greedily eat the food being offered. As they consume it, however, they will gradually become less active and this is the point at which to stop feeding. This will avoid overfeeding and the problems of polluting the aquarium.

Some owners prefer to soak pellet foods before offering them to their goldfish. This not only softens the food, but also stops it from floating on the surface. Fancy varieties may suffer from swimbladder disorders (see page 15) and soaking the food may help to reduce the likelihood of this happening because the food is softer and the fish do not need to gape at the surface to feed. Avoid soaking the food for more than about a minute, otherwise water-soluble vitamins such as ascorbic acid (vitamin C) will begin to leach out. Bear in mind that some kinds of food are not suitable for soaking in water and will disintegrate.

FEEDING GOLDFISH

Feeding goldfish

In addition to proprietary diets, goldfish appreciate the occasional treat food. Manufactured treat foods are available in tablet form. Natural foods are always popular and very good for getting adult goldfish into breeding condition. Frozen foods, such as bloodworm, chopped mussels and brineshrimp, are suitable, but always thaw them out first. Once thawed, give them to the fish straightaway. Goldfish can also be offered pieces of orange and lettuce leaves to browse on, but remove any uneaten food before it can pollute the water.

▲ Goldfish will eat small shrimps and other live foods as part of their diet.

Daphnia (water fleas)

Brineshrimp

Bloodworms (midge larvae)

STORING FOOD

Always store supplies of manufactured food in dry conditions in an airtight container. Only buy as much food as will be eaten within a few weeks of opening. It is false economy to buy in bulk, as the vitamin content of the food begins to break down once the container has been opened. After a few weeks, the vitamin content is negligible and the food is thus of little nutritive value. If food becomes damp, discard it, as the moisture encourages moulds, which are poisonous to goldfish.

Frozen irradiated bloodworms.

Once defrosted, they are an excellent food.

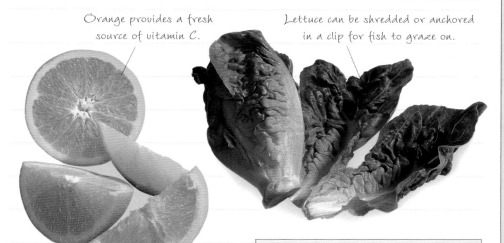

Orange provides a fresh source of vitamin C.

Lettuce can be shredded or anchored in a clip for fish to graze on.

▼ *At holiday time, an autofeeder – a timer-controlled reservoir for flake or small granules – dispenses one or more meals daily.*

Feeding blocks slowly dissolve.

HOLIDAY FEEDING

Another cause for concern is what to do about feeding your goldfish while you are on holiday. There are various ways of tackling this problem. One method is to buy 'vacation blocks', which contain food in a compressed block that gradually dissolves, allowing the fish to eat the food. Alternatively, during the two weeks leading up to your holiday, gradually reduce the amount of food you offer until on the day of departure you stop feeding the fish altogether. On your return, gradually start feeding the goldfish again, so that after 10-14 days they are consuming their normal quantity of food. Many people prefer to ask a neighbour or friend to look after the aquarium in their absence. Measure out the daily food ration into individual plastic bags to avoid keen volunteers offering too much food, which may lead to water quality problems.

Breeding goldfish

It can be quite difficult to differentiate between the sexes of both common and fancy goldfish. Usually, the female has a much rounder appearance, due to the development of eggs in the ovaries. Male fish often develop tubercles – also called a spawning rash – when they are in breeding condition. The female lays her eggs and the male swims immediately behind, shedding milt (sperm). The eggs stick to plant leaves, whether fertilised or not.

▼ *The male (left) Redcap Oranda shows tubercles on the gill covers. The female lays her eggs in dense aquatic vegetation.*

* Males and females are best kept in separate tanks to condition them before spawning.

▲ *The tubercles can be seen as raised white pimples on the gill covers of male fish. Do not confuse them with the disease whitespot.*

SPEED OF HATCHING

The speed with with goldfish embryos develop depends on the water temperature, and hatching can take between six and seven days at 16°C (61°F), three days at about 25°C (77°F) and just two days at 30°C (86°F). In the controlled temperature of an aquarium (between 22 and 23°C/72-74°F), the young goldfish should hatch in four to four-and-a-half days.

▼ *Immediately after hatching, the tiny larvae with large eyes feed on the remains of the yolk and then swim to the surface.*

MAKING A SPAWNING MOP

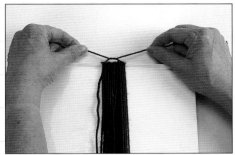

1 In the aquarium, eggs can adhere to a spawning mop. Wind green nylon wool about 30 times around a book. Cut off the surplus.

2 Thread another piece of wool about 20cm (8in) long under the strands and secure the strands with a tight knot.

3 Turn over the book and cut the wool strands at the point opposite your knot. Do not cut off the long ends securing the strands. Wash the mop in warm water before the first use. Before reusing a mop, dry it out and wash it again.

Green is a natural colour.

4 Here, the long ends are attached to a cork to keep it at the water surface. Alternatively, suspend the mop by the long ends from the surface. Use one or more mops in the tank.

Breeding goldfish

Controlled spawning allows you to select the broodstock (parent fish) and, therefore, the production of fry with desirable colour or characteristics. Equip the largest possible tank with a simple sponge filter, as larvae or fry could be sucked into filter mechanisms. Condition the broodstock with a high-protein diet, plus live food, and keep the water at 20°C (68°F). Partial water changes may help to trigger spawning. After spawning, remove the parents to prevent them eating the eggs.

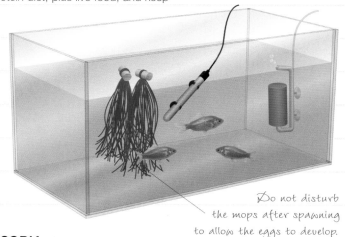

▶ *Place two males and one female in the tank. They should spawn within a few days.*

Do not disturb the mops after spawning to allow the eggs to develop.

CULTIVATING INFUSORIA

◀ *To culture infusoria – an ideal fry food – place a piece of lightly boiled potato in a jar of tank water.*

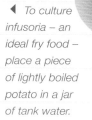

▲ *These nine-week-old Red Metallic Ranchus already have a good body shape, but the hood may take three years to develop. Continue feeding heavily.*

▶ *After a week or so in a warm spot, the jar will be cloudy with infusoria. Pour some into the tank.*

MAKING A WORMERY

Earthworms, chopped or fed whole, are protein-packed and excellent for conditioning parent fish before they spawn. To collect your own worms, dig over a shady corner of the garden and cover a patch of soil with one or two hessian sacks. Keep these well-watered and seed them with all your used teabags and soft food scraps. Worms will congregate under the sacks and can be picked off the surface – much easier than spadework!

CULTURING MICROWORMS

▲ To culture microworms, place a spoonful of old culture onto the new medium. Keep it away from the kitchen, as it can be smelly.

CULTURING BRINESHRIMP

Dried brineshrimp eggs in sealed containers are available from aquatic outlets. Keep them in cool, dry conditions, or they will fail to hatch.

1 Hatching the fine brineshrimp eggs is easy. Half-fill a one-litre bottle with fresh tap water, add one-and-a-half teaspoons of sea salt and a quarter of a teaspoon of eggs.

Well-washed plastic drinks bottle with airline shown below.

Aquarium salt.

Use only a small quantity of eggs at a time.

2 Drop in an airline attached to an airpump. The bubbles will circulate the eggs in the bottle. Rigid airline is best but flexible tubing works if properly positioned.

3 After 36 hours, remove the airline and 30 minutes later siphon out the shrimps, filter them through paper towel, wash them in freshwater and feed them to the fry.

BREEDING GOLDFISH

Health care

Keeping goldfish is a rewarding hobby, but as with any other pet animals, there are occasions when they become sick. It is sad to realise that the commonest reasons for goldfish to become sick are attributable to inadequate management, resulting in bad water conditions. As a consequence, the fish become stressed and prone to any number of secondary diseases.

SYMPTOMS TO LOOK FOR

White pimples on the skin are clear signs of a parasitic condition called whitespot.

The delicate tissue between fin rays can become eroded by fin rot, a bacterial disease.

Areas of redness or ulcers are caused by bacterial infection.

In fish with dropsy, the scales protrude from the body surface like a pinecone.

▶ *Advanced stages of fin rot are clearly visible on this goldfish. This often occurs as a secondary stage of other diseases or in fish that are stressed by overcrowding or poor water.*

▲ *A reddened bacterial ulcer and raised scales will need antibiotic treatment.*

◀ *The excess mucus shown here could be caused by poor water conditions or a severe parasitic infection.*

Prompt action is needed to save this goldfish.

▼ *Goldfish suffering from swimbladder disorders appear to lose their balance and have difficulty staying upright in the water.*

A cyst or tumour is common, but will not spread to others or impair the affected fish.

KEEPING A RECORD

It is a good idea to keep a written record of the results of any water tests and to note details of water changes, such as how much water was changed and when. Use the record book to note changes in the behaviour of any of the goldfish, as these might indicate the start of a health problem. Writing down these details will draw attention to imminent problems and, hopefully, your response will be a case of prevention rather than cure.

Health care

In the event of an outbreak of disease, it is important to diagnose the problem accurately and to apply the correct medication. If you are not sure what to do, seek professional help, rather than use a range of medications that may not work and could even aggravate the situation. When using any medication, be sure to follow the directions exactly and measure any treatment carefully. Never be tempted to add a few extra drops of any medication on the basis that a bit more than directed can only be helpful. Many of these treatments are very potent and even a small excess could be sufficient to overdose the affected fish.

1 Fill a plastic jug with tank water and add the medication to it.

2 Thoroughly mix the medication into the water. Diluting it first reduces the risk of producing localised spots of dangerously high concentrations.

3 Gently introduce the diluted medication into the tank. Remember to keep any utensils solely for aquarium use.

NEW TANK SYNDROME

The commonest health pitfall – and one that occurs in the early stages of running in an aquarium – arises from being in too much of a hurry to stock it with fish. This 'new tank syndrome' is more accurately known as ammonia or nitrite poisoning and can be avoided by frequent water testing and carrying out partial water changes.

◀ Healthy gills, showing the central primary lamella and the thin-walled secondary lamellae.

◀ High ammonia levels have thickened the secondary lamellae, reducing the surface area.

QUARANTINE OR HOSPITAL TANK

A heater set to 18°C (64°F) prevents fluctuations in temperature.

An internal filter will control fish waste and maintain water quality.

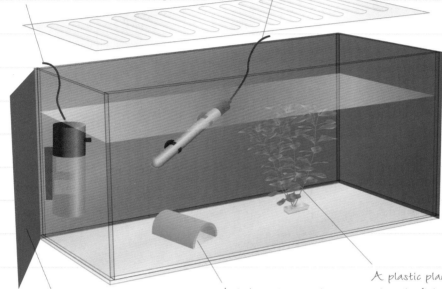

Screen the back and sides to make the tank darker and more tranquil.

A hiding place, such as a piece of pipe, provides reassurance for the fish.

A plastic plant makes the fish feel at home and is easy to keep clean.

◀ Aeration in treatment tanks can enhance oxygen uptake and carbon dioxide loss at the water surface.

* Keep a note of the volume of water in your tank so that you can dose the tank accurately with tonics or medications.

EUTHANASIA

Sometimes a goldfish becomes so sick that it is better to euthanase it than allow it to endure a lingering death. The kindest way is to mix a minimum of 10 drops of clove oil per litre of tank water in a container before introducing the goldfish. If you feel you cannot do this yourself, consult a veterinarian.

▲ *Two young London Shubunkins with characteristic calico coloration. With no reflective guanine pigment in and beneath the scales, the skin appears matt. In the best show fish, blue should be dominant.*

* To the Chinese, goldfish represent wealth and prosperity. To ensure success, business owners will keep a collection of fancy goldfish on the premises as a good luck charm.

GOLDFISH VARIETIES

A multitude of fancy varieties has been developed from the humble beginnings of the ancestral goldfish; indeed, it is thought that over 120 varieties of fancy goldfish have been developed and each season brings with it new and sometimes (though not always) highly attractive varieties. Firstly, the tail fin became paired, and in some cases, the lack of a dorsal fin, skyward-looking eyes, or both, were developed as a characteristic. Additional characteristics, such as the fluffy 'hood' prized by enthusiasts of the Oranda, Lionhead and Ranchu, also became popular.

At the same time, variations in colouring have been developed, with the result that goldfish varieties now range from matt black through blue, chocolate brown and orange-speckled to silver with a scarlet 'cap'. It is not unusual to see goldfish with an attractive red-and-silver, or sarasa, colouring. This has traditionally been the popular colouring of the Comet goldfish.

In addition to colour, fish with different scale types have been developed. One of the most notable is the Pearlscale, which has convex or domed scales. These, combined with a virtually spherical body shape, give the fish the appearance of an oversized golf ball.

Recent introductions include the Panda Butterfly, an extremely elegant black-and-silver fancy goldfish with globe-shaped eyes and a tail resembling a butterfly. The Japanese have successfully developed the Jikin (pronounced jee-kin). This all-silver, metallic variety has the body shape of the ancestral goldfish and a most attractive red colouring, ideally restricted to the fins and lips.

Common goldfish

A good-quality Common goldfish should have a body shape similar to that of its wild-type ancestors. That is, a body depth of no more than three-eighths of its body length, excluding the tail, and a gently curved dorsal profile. The length of the body should be slightly more than twice the depth and the dorsal profile gently curved. The pectoral and pelvic fins are paired and the dorsal, caudal (tail) and anal fins should be single. The caudal fin should be short and stumpy, and all the other fins should be rounded and like little paddles. Common goldfish are metallic and can be either all one colour (self-coloured) or a combination of colours (variegated).

▼ *Look for a sturdy body with a smooth outline.*

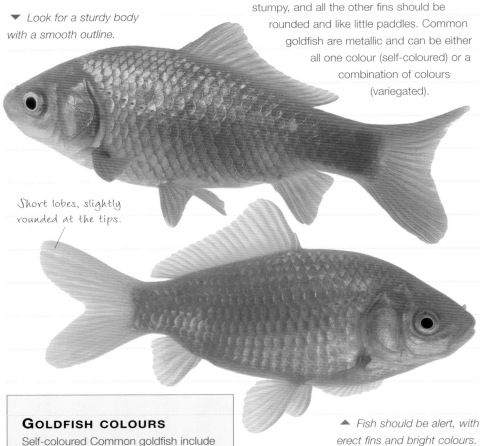

Short lobes, slightly rounded at the tips.

▲ *Fish should be alert, with erect fins and bright colours.*

GOLDFISH COLOURS

Self-coloured Common goldfish include red, orange, yellow, blue, brown, and black. Variegated Common goldfish also include silver in different combinations. The patterns should be balanced and clear, and extend into the fins.

* Common goldfish are farm-reared for the 'pet' market. Hobbyists focus on breeding high-quality specimens.

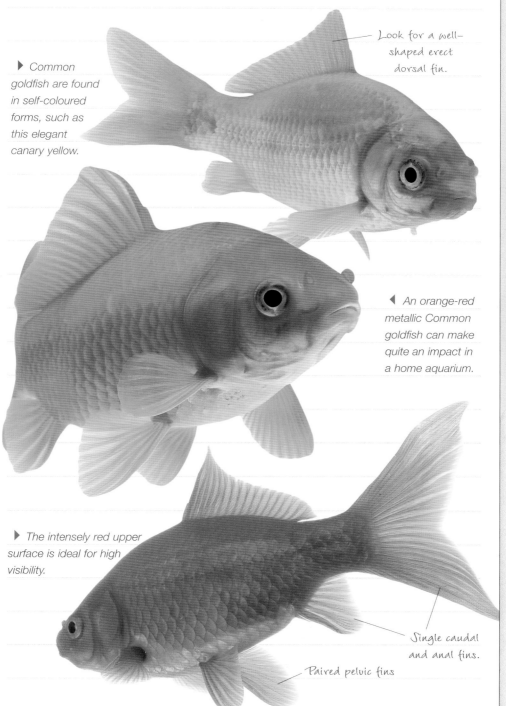

Look for a well-shaped erect dorsal fin.

▶ Common goldfish are found in self-coloured forms, such as this elegant canary yellow.

◀ An orange-red metallic Common goldfish can make quite an impact in a home aquarium.

▶ The intensely red upper surface is ideal for high visibility.

Single caudal and anal fins.

Paired pelvic fins

COMMON GOLDFISH

Comet goldfish

The features of a good Comet are like those of a first-rate Common goldfish, but with a more slender body. Generally, the fins are longer and more elegant than those of the Common goldfish, but the main difference is in the caudal fin, which is deeply forked and must be at least half (ideally three-quarters) the length of the body.

One of the most popular variegated colours is the Sarasa Comet – red and silver.

The lobes of the caudal fin should be clearly pointed at the tips and held spread, without folding or overlapping.

▶ *The colour should be intense and extend into the fins.*

* Comets were first bred in the United States during the late 1800s.

▼ *These active young Sarasa Comets are constantly on the move.*

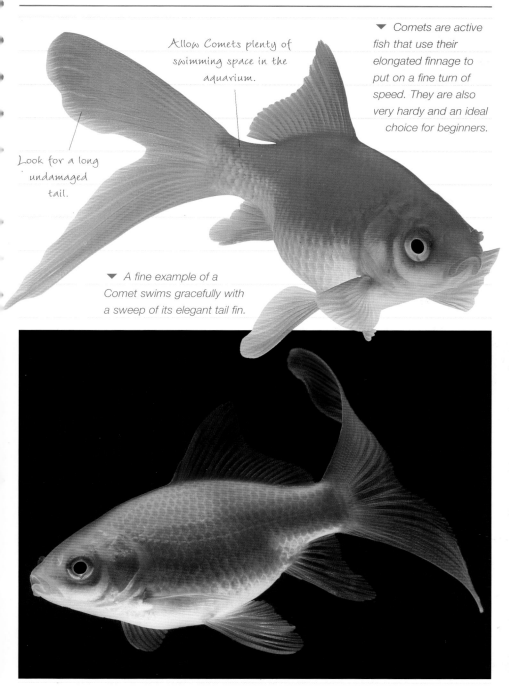

Allow Comets plenty of swimming space in the aquarium.

Look for a long undamaged tail.

▼ Comets are active fish that use their elongated finnage to put on a fine turn of speed. They are also very hardy and an ideal choice for beginners.

▼ A fine example of a Comet swims gracefully with a sweep of its elegant tail fin.

COMET GOLDFISH

Shubunkin

The Shubunkin is another popular single-tailed variety, typically with calico (multicoloured) markings. Blue is an important shade and for show-quality fish, at least 25% of the body must be of this colour. The blue should form the background colour and there should be areas of violet, red, orange, yellow and brown. Finally, there should be an even distribution of black spots. There are two varieties of Shubunkin, the London (identical in body shape and finnage to a Common goldfish) and the Bristol (with longer and more developed fins).

▼ *Colour should extend right into the boundaries of the tail, as shown here.*

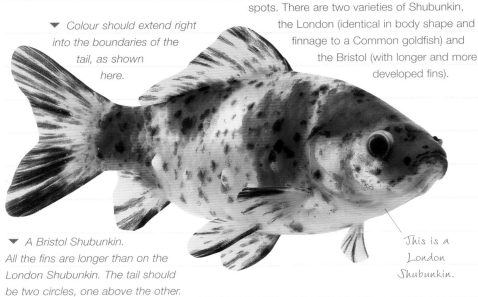

This is a London Shubunkin.

▼ *A Bristol Shubunkin. All the fins are longer than on the London Shubunkin. The tail should be two circles, one above the other.*

▼ A good example, with no hump on the dorsal region and nicely rounded mouth.

▼ Here the body and fins are good, but ideally the blotches of red should be smaller.

▶ A lovely example of a London Shubunkin. A well-balanced fish with very good finnage and body shape. Nice colours, although a little too blotchy when judged by show standards.

Fantail

The body of the Fantail is deep – at least three-fifths of the body length. The dorsal fin is single, and all the other fins should be paired and have slightly rounded tips. The caudal fin should be both divided and forked and is the major characteristic of the variety. As the fish swims, the caudal fin should not drop or fold and, when viewed from above, should have a fan shape. Originally, standards were set for two different variations of the caudal fin – a longer, finer, flowing tail, or a shorter and rather stumpy tail. However, rather than keeping them separate, these have been amalgamated to a single standard for the Fantail variety.

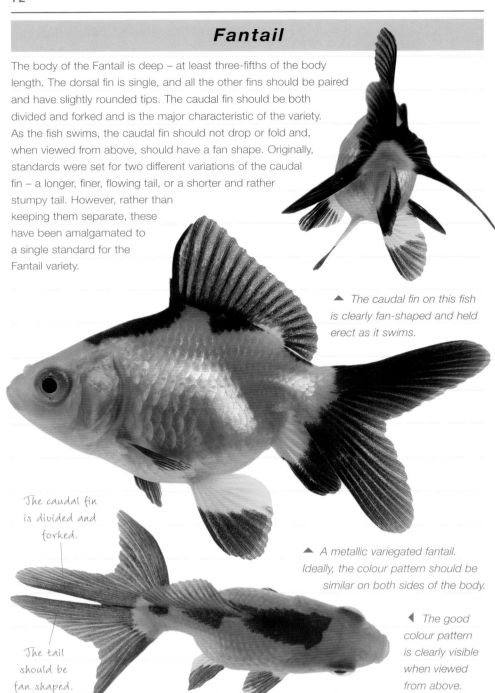

▲ The caudal fin on this fish is clearly fan-shaped and held erect as it swims.

The caudal fin is divided and forked.

The tail should be fan shaped.

▲ A metallic variegated fantail. Ideally, the colour pattern should be similar on both sides of the body.

◀ The good colour pattern is clearly visible when viewed from above.

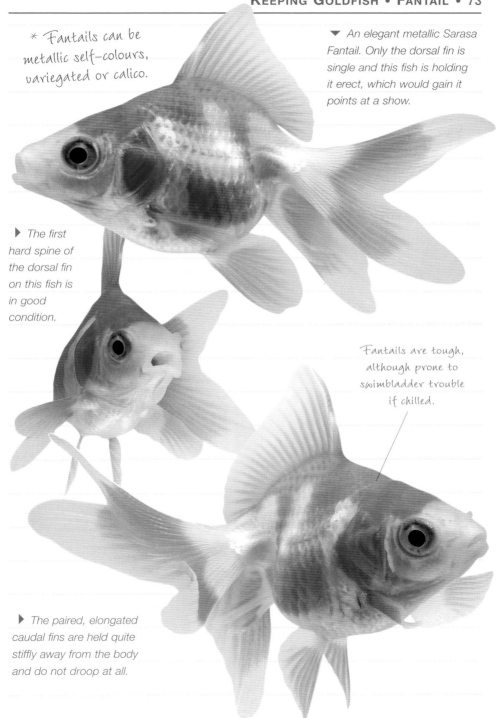

* Fantails can be metallic self-colours, variegated or calico.

▼ An elegant metallic Sarasa Fantail. Only the dorsal fin is single and this fish is holding it erect, which would gain it points at a show.

▶ The first hard spine of the dorsal fin on this fish is in good condition.

Fantails are tough, although prone to swimbladder trouble if chilled.

▶ The paired, elongated caudal fins are held quite stiffly away from the body and do not droop at all.

Veiltail

The Veiltail has a short body, the depth of which should be no more than two-thirds the length. The dorsal fin – the only single fin – is long, its height being roughly two-thirds of the body depth. The pectorals, and in particular the pelvic fins, should be long and narrow. The paired caudal fin is the prominent feature of this variety and should be flowing and long, at least three-quarters of the body length. The caudal fin should not be forked or have pointed lobes but should be divided when viewing the fish from above. As a Veiltail swims, the dorsal fin should be upright and flow rather like a flag, without bending or sagging. The caudal fin should flow gracefully. Calico or metallic self-coloured and variegated forms of Veiltail are acceptable, but the colours must be strong and extend into the fins.

▼ *This calico Veiltail has a flowing tail fin with an ideal squared-off trailing edge.*

▲ A red metallic Veiltail with the typical high dorsal fin and long, narrow pelvic and pectoral fins. The flowing fins are easily damaged, so it is best to keep Veiltails with other long-finned varieties.

* Good-quality Veiltails conforming to the required standard are difficult to breed. Pairs often fail to produce offspring similar to the parental variety.

Ryukin

The Ryukin is regarded as a Japanese variety of goldfish, supposedly having arrived there via the Ryukyu Islands, which lie between Japan and Taiwan. The Ryukin is a very popular fish in Japan and is quite large, attaining a size of about 20cm (8in). The body is deep, and the back slopes up steeply from behind the head, which is long and distinctly pointed in shape. The dorsal fin is high and the long tail fin may have either three or four lobes. The three-lobed tail should have a slight indentation, which is known in Japan as the 'cherry blossom petal tail'. The Ryukin can be self-coloured metallic, variegated or calico.

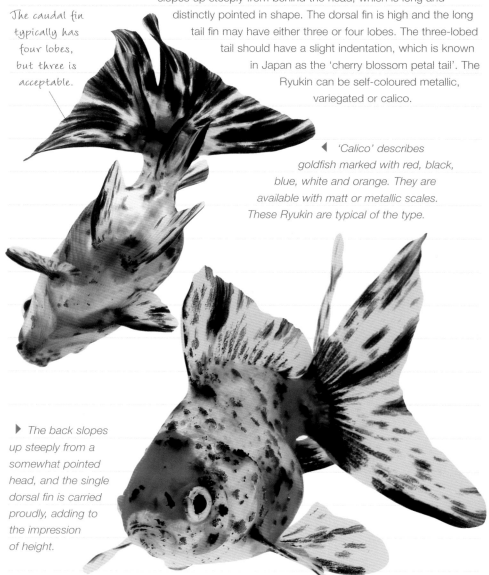

The caudal fin typically has four lobes, but three is acceptable.

◀ *'Calico' describes goldfish marked with red, black, blue, white and orange. They are available with matt or metallic scales. These Ryukin are typical of the type.*

▶ *The back slopes up steeply from a somewhat pointed head, and the single dorsal fin is carried proudly, adding to the impression of height.*

▶ Red-and-silver Ryukins such as this are regarded by the Japanese as the best examples of the variety. The pattern should be balanced and the red should be a rich deep colour, as shown here.

Look for a well-shaped tail.

There is a noticeable hump behind the head.

▼ Two further examples of red-and-silver Ryukins show how the pattern can vary. These Ryukin are typical of the matt type.

RYUKIN

Oranda

The Oranda has a short body, the depth of which is roughly two-thirds the length. The dorsal fin should be single and high, with all other fins paired and long. The caudal fins should be divided, and current standards call for the trailing edge of the tail to be more like the square edge of the Moor and Veiltail.

▼ *The hood develops from white spots and a filmy covering in three areas: the top of the head, around the eyes and around the gills.*

▲ *Three young Orandas. At this early stage, look for a generous width across the head between the eyes, making a good platform for hood development.*

▶ *The black markings on this young fish look attractive, but are only temporary and will become totally red in time.*

▲ Different colour combinations in young Orandas.

* In Orandas bred in the Far East, the trailing edge of the caudal fins is deeply forked.

▲ A high dorsal fin and long, veiltail-type caudal fins are typical features of Orandas.

▼ The body shape shows clearly in this view. Orandas are not the easiest fish to keep and need a good varied diet.

The hood growth may obscure the eyes.

Oranda

The main characteristic of the Oranda is the development of wartlike excrescences to form a wen, or hood, on the head. In good specimens, each of the little rounded excrescences should be of the same size. Recently, the Chinese have bred Orandas with telescope eyes.

In addition to metallic, self-coloured, variegated and calico colour types, there is a separate category for the Redcap Oranda. In this variety, as the name suggests, the hood is a deep red and should be confined to the crown of the head, while the body should be silver. Among the metallic and calico varieties, the hood should cover the top of the head, extending around the eye and onto the gill covers.

◀ *A red hood on a red fish shows the two shades that can result from the presence or absence of scales. On the metallic body the colour is more orange, while the head (with no scales) is more crimson.*

▼ *As it swims, the fins of the Oranda should flow gracefully.*

▼ Redcap Orandas are so called because of the colour of the hood. The Japanese like these goldfish because the marking mimics that on the head of their national bird, the Tancho crane.

▲ In Redcap Orandas, the hood is confined to the top of the head, where each warty element should be of equal size.

* In the West, specimens of Oranda with a forked tail can be shown but points will be deducted for this feature.

This finnage is of the Veiltail type.

▲ The body should be silver and the finnage pure white, with no red intruding.

Moor • Globe-eye

A Moor is a black Veiltail with globe-eyes, and although perfect examples are hard to find, the variety is enduringly popular. Moors should be a uniform velvety black, but bronze scalation tends to show through with age. The overall body shape of the Globe-eye is similar to that of the Veiltail, with a single dorsal fin and pointed tips to the other fins, all of which should be paired. The eyes protrude from the head. The caudal fin should be forked to about a quarter of its length, and long – about three-quarters of the body length.

* All fancies of this general shape require a deep tank — 50cm/ 20in minimum — to give them sufficient swimming space.

▲ The flowing single dorsal and other paired fins lend this short-bodied fish a certain grace.

▶ The Moor's eyes should be spherical overall. They should be large and protrude from the head, almost as if they were stuck to the surface.

The eyes should be at the tip of truncated cone-shaped protuberances and should be symmetrical.

* The Globe-eye is also known as the Telescope-eye in the USA and the Dragon Fish in the Far East.

▲ A red-and-black Globe-eye in good condition, showing a high and upright dorsal fin and very good body shape.

▼ An attractive calico Globe-eye displaying the deep body, erect single dorsal fin and the other (paired) fins.

▲ The protruding eyes are clearly visible in this view.

Calico colours should be bright and on a blue background.

Butterfly

As the name implies, the Panda Butterfly is black and white (silver). Ideally, the colouring should be intensely black and like polished silver in a well-balanced pattern on either side of the body. The eyes are similar to those of the Moor. Another feature of this variety is the butterfly tail. When buying Panda Butterfly goldfish, look for bright, alert specimens, with all their fins well spread. This variety is very similar to the Globe-eye.

▶ *The Panda Butterfly, sometimes also known as the Magpie, is one of the newer varieties and gaining in popularity.*

▼ *The silver-and-black pattern is highly variable, but when dark globe-eyes appear on a white face the 'panda' illusion is complete.*

Mainly white, this is still a fine Panda Butterfly.

▲ *From this angle it is clear that the caudal fin of this young specimen is only 25% divided. Ideally, it should be fully divided.*

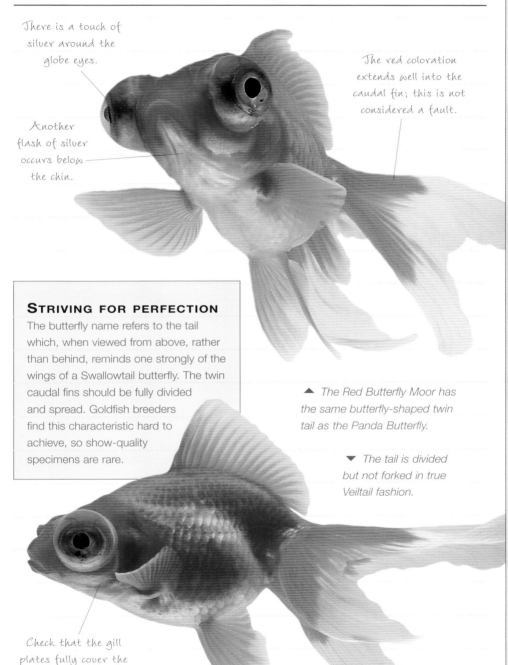

There is a touch of silver around the globe eyes.

Another flash of silver occurs below the chin.

The red coloration extends well into the caudal fin; this is not considered a fault.

STRIVING FOR PERFECTION

The butterfly name refers to the tail which, when viewed from above, rather than behind, reminds one strongly of the wings of a Swallowtail butterfly. The twin caudal fins should be fully divided and spread. Goldfish breeders find this characteristic hard to achieve, so show-quality specimens are rare.

▲ The Red Butterfly Moor has the same butterfly-shaped twin tail as the Panda Butterfly.

▼ The tail is divided but not forked in true Veiltail fashion.

Check that the gill plates fully cover the delicate gills beneath.

Ranchu

The Ranchu is very similar in appearance to the Chinese Lionhead. However, the back is strongly arched, forming a sharp angle with the caudal fin and as a result, the caudal fin is orientated downwards. The absence of a dorsal fin, the shape of the other paired fins, and the hood are all similar to those of the Lionhead. Ranchus are bred in metallic self-coloration or combinations, as well as calico.

▲ This is an excellent specimen of a black Ranchu, a variety highly prized by the Japanese.

◀ In red-and-silver metallic Ranchu, the twin coloration can flow across the body in an informal pattern.

The red wen, or hood.

▶ The markings resemble those of a Kohaku (red-and-white) koi.

RANCHU

The tail fin faces downwards.

▶ A top view reveals the strong and chunky body of this fine red metallic Ranchu.

▶ A side view of the Ranchu shown above it. Note the clean angle of the back.

◀ In this red-and-silver metallic Ranchu, the red hood covers the top of the head, spreads around the eyes and extends over the gill covers.

An ideal 90° angle.

▶ The most obvious feature of the Ranchu profile is the steeply arched back and absence of the dorsal fin.

A fine example of the breed.

Pompon

The Pompon has a body shape and arrangement of fins similar to that described for the Celestial and Bubble-eye. Fish have two nostrils on either side of the head, interconnected by a U-shaped tube lined with sensory cells that can detect very small amounts of dissolved chemicals in the water. A tiny flap of skin, called the nasal septum, separates the two orifices that form the nostrils. In the Pompon, the nasal septa have been developed into bunches of fleshy lobes that resemble pompons.

In good-quality Pompons, the lobes are of equal size.

▶ *Note the good contrast in coloration between the nasal growths and the rest of the body in these Chocolate Pompons.*

▼ *Calico Pompons should have a blue background with patches of colour and be spotted with black. This Lionhead type has no dorsal fin.*

POMPON

* The function of the nostrils is rather like that of the human nose, giving fish the ability to smell chemicals or odours.

▲ Pompons are found in both metallic (here, red) and calico colour forms.

The pompons should be well developed but not sucked into the mouth as the fish breathes.

▶ Pompons can be of the Fantail type, with a dorsal fin, as shown here.

Hama Nishiki • Pearlscale

Hama Nishiki is a cross between the Pearlscale and the Oranda. The body shape and scales of the Hama Nishiki are essentially like those of the Pearlscale. The dorsal fin is single and all the others are paired, but slightly longer on the Hama Nishiki than the Pearlscale. The main characteristic that distinguishes the Hama Nishiki from a Pearlscale is the presence of a wen (hood) covering the top of the head. Overall, the Hama Nishiki is slightly larger than the Pearlscale, growing to about 20cm (8in) long.

▲ Look for good pearling, well-balanced finnage and a pointed head.

▲ The dome-shaped scales are clear to see, as is the hood, which will probably develop further as the fish matures.

The body is deep and broad.

▶ In this Hama Nishiki, the fins are longer than those of the Pearlscale, but this is not always the case.

◀ *The Pearlscale's forked and divided tail is carried high. Other characteristics include a rather dainty head and small mouth.*

* In the Pearlscale, each scale is thickened in the centre with a deposit of calcium carbonate (chalk) that makes it stand proud.

▲ *The raised scales look like dimples on a golf ball. The body is almost spherical.*

▶ *A young red-and-white Pearlscale, showing the calcium deposits beneath the scales.*

Celestial

The Celestial tends to be one of the smaller varieties of fancy goldfish. The dorsal fin is absent and the back is gently sloping towards the caudal fin, which should be clearly divided and forked. All the other fins are paired and should have rounded edges. The body is deep, ideally at least half the body length, but the notable feature concerns the eyes, which not only protrude but face upwards. These spherical protuberances should be well developed and in good specimens of Celestial are the same size, shape and coloration. The Celestial and Bubble-eye did not appear until the eighteenth century. The origins of the Celestial are shrouded in mystery, with some suggestion that this variety was obtained by the Chinese from Korea. Celestials begin life looking much like other goldfish, but the eyes soon start to migrate around the head until they are facing directly upwards. The recessive gene causing this feature would never have survived long in nature.

AQUARIUM CARE

Celestials should be kept in an aquarium without strong lighting or any tank decor on which they might injure their delicate eye tissue. For this reason they are probably not suitable for the novice fishkeeper.

* The first fancy goldfish were kept in opaque ceramic bowls, when direct eye contact with their owners was possible only with this variety.

▼ The eyes of the Celestial not only protrude but must look upwards. In good-quality fish, they are equal in size.

* Celestials occur as metallic self-coloured, variegated, and calico fish.

▲ The Celestial has no dorsal fin, but should show a smoothly arched back, as here. The caudal fins should not be too big or the body too long and shallow.

Bubble-eye

The Bubble-eye's body shape and arrangement of fins are similar to that described for the Celestial, but its distinguishing feature, as the name suggests, is the extreme development of fluid-filled pouches of skin under and around the eyes. Viewed from the side, the Bubble-eye looks rather as if it is peeping over the top of the bubblelike pouches. As it swims, the pouches wobble in a characteristic fashion. In very good specimens of Bubble-eye, the pouches are well developed and of a similar size and shape. Bubble-eyes may be calico or metallic self-coloured and variegated. The skin surrounding the bubble-like pouch is easily damaged, particularly if internal filters are used in the aquarium. Keep the fish in a bare tank with no plants, sharp gravel or ornaments on which it could injure itself. This is not a fish for the novice fishkeeper.

▶ *In the Bubble-eye, the dorsal fin is absent and the body should be smoothly contoured.*

▶ *The delicate 'bubble' is a fluid-filled pouch, or sac, that protrudes from beneath each eye.*

▼ An example of a self-coloured metallic bronze Bubble-eye with good eye development.

* Since these fish tend to be poor swimmers, they are best kept in a separate aquarium.

The tail should be divided and forked.

▲ Orange Bubble-eyes, like their bronze counterparts, can attain a mature size of 20cm (8in) in an aquarium where they do not need to compete for food.

▶ The eyes do not protrude, but, like those of the Celestials, they look upwards and are situated above the fluid-filled pouches.

These pouches are equal in size – a good feature.

BUBBLE-EYE

Picture credits

Additional picture credits

The publishers would like to thank the following photographers for providing images, credited here by page number and position: T(Top), B(Bottom), C(Centre), BL(Bottom Left), etc.

Aqua Press (M-P & C Piednoir): 36(TR), 60(BR, Peter Cole)

Dave Bevan: 54(TR), 60(BL), 61(T,B), 92
Dick Mills: 8(T)
Arend van den Nieuwenhuizen 56(CL)
Mike Pepper: 8(B)
Photomax (Max Gibbs): 56(BR), 70(B), 74, 75, 88(B), 89(T), 91(BR), 93
Reef One Ltd: 20
Neil Sutherland © Interpet Publishing: 5(TL), 6(T), 21(T), 45(C,B), 53(B), 96